VOICES IN THE RAIN FOREST

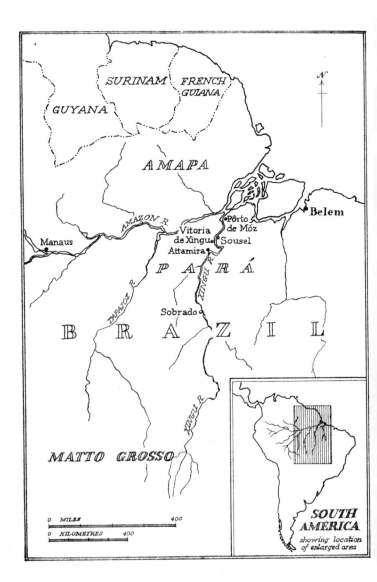

VOICES
IN THE
RAIN FOREST

by
HORACE BANNER

Illustrations by
MONICA YOUNG

LUTTERWORTH PRESS · LONDON

First published 1971

Published by Lutterworth Press, 4 Bouverie Street,
London, E.C.4,
on behalf of
The Unevangelized Fields Mission,
9 Gunnersbury Avenue, London, W.5,
and 306 Bala Avenue, Bala Cynwyd, Pa.19004, U.S.A.

ISBN 0 7188 1774 5

COPYRIGHT © 1971 HORACE BANNER

Printed in Great Britain
at the St. Ann's Press, Park Road, Altrincham

CONTENTS

FOREWORD

The address below is that of the headquarters in Brazil of the Unevangelized Fields Mission, with whom I work as a missionary.

Brasil—spelt on the spot with *s* instead of *z*, is the biggest country in South America and fourth largest in the world.

Pará is the name of a State. The accent on the *a* indicates that it takes all the emphasis. It is as though you were saying Pa-rat with the *t* crossed out. There are twenty-one States in Brazil and Pará is the third biggest, and nine times the size of England and Wales.

Belem—the Brazilian way of writing Bethlehem—is the Capital of Pará State, a modern city with a sprouting sky-line, one-way streets seething with traffic and plenty of noise and bustle. Situated right at the mouth of the River Amazon, with several miles of docks, its position gives it tremendous strategic importance.

Caixa—pronounced *kye-sha*—stands for post-office box.

Now, although these stories were posted at the branch post-office just two hundred yards from the Mission House, they were actually written in various places on the Xingu River—I'll refer to it as the *River X* to avoid problems of pronunciation—which flows into the Amazon after cutting its way through over a thousand miles of rain forest.

Caixa 243,   HORACE BANNER.
Belem-Pará,
Brasil.

1

VOICES IN THE RAIN FOREST

IN THE WILDS of the River X, life can still be very much what it was almost five centuries ago when white men first discovered what they called the New World. In forests, which from an airplane look like a vast green billiard table or an ocean of interwoven tree tops, there are tribes of primitive Indians who live in a jungle world of bows and arrows, paint and feathers, wooden sword-clubs and stone axes, who still make fire by rubbing one stick into another. What we call civilization has made little more than a finger mark on them.

Planes may fly overhead, from time to time the pounding of the diesel engine of a trader's launch navigating a rapids-strewn river, or shots from a hunter's rifle may invade the domain of the forest's wild life, but the voice of the rain forest is that of the thunderstorms which may darken the skies on over a hundred days each year, crashing timbers, bird cries, animal calls and the wheeling, whirring, whistling and chirping of insects.

These are the sounds I hear in the junglelands which for many years have been home to me and my family. To the Indians, I am *Orat*, the nearest they can get to my name. Donna Eva is my wife. Our two children, Jess and Jim, spent their early years in our forest home, though for schooling they had to go to the Mission boarding school in Belem, and then to England.

They are always as happy to come "home" to us for their holidays, as we ourselves are to get away from the noisy outside world the moment whatever business takes us to the city can be completed.

During inevitable periods of waiting in Belem, as we make yearly or half-yearly purchases of stores and equipment, or visit doctor or dentist, there is nothing we like better than to slip away for an hour to a small "island" or virgin forest within easy reach of the Mission House and City Centre, a carefully preserved memorial of the time when what is now a marvellous capital city was just as much rain forest as our home on the River X still is. Behind a fringe of giant trees and an undergrowth of ferns and palms, and still within range of the noise of passing traffic, are the Pará Botanical and Zoological Gardens. The Zoo is not a big one but it is unique in that everything there—animals, birds, reptiles and fish—are native to the forests of the Amazon region.

Crocodiles and boa-constrictors laze in near-natural surroundings. Emus (the South American brand of ostrich) strut around with heads high up in the air, and, thanks to the periscope of a neck with which Nature has provided them, are able to look down on mere visitors like ourselves. Jaguars growl. Red macaw parrots squawk. Armadillos burrow and anteaters sleep under their blanket-like tails. Giant tortoises share a pen with red deer and grey tapirs. There are playful monkeys which chatter and glum ones which howl—according to their species. Sloths and wild boar, leopard cats and porcupines, herons and peacocks, cranes and flamingoes, they are all there. Through the glass panels of the aquarium, we can see the killer fish we call piranha being fed, or watch the electric eels.

Life in the wilds of the River X has given us close-up contacts with many of these jungle creatures in their

10

natural setting, away from all the pens and cages. Not all of them are in the "All things bright and beautiful" class. Some may not even be either "wise or wonderful" at first sight, but we have lived long enough to see that everything has its purpose.

"Ask the beasts and they shall teach thee," wrote the observant Job. Following his wise and ancient advice, we have kept eyes and ears open and seek to pass on some of what we have learned.

2

SERPENT IN THE RIVER

Here we have cloudless skies for five months each year and—if we feel like it—swimming every day. Except when the river is in flood because of the heavy rains, we have a lovely beach within easy reach of our home.

Early each morning the women go down to the river to fill their clay water-pots and calabashes before the water is disturbed by all the coming and going the day will bring. The men have their little dug-outs moored to pegs driven deep into the sand. Out in the shallows are several table-like contraptions—heavy boards perched on forked sticks—where the women sit in the water while rubbing soap over dirty clothes and then banging out the dirt as they bring the soaking garments swishing down on the table tops. Fish scales on a big, flat stone mark the place where the fishermen's wives and daughters clean the day's catch and prepare it for the cooking pot. The entrails they throw into deep water where lurk the ever-hungry piranha fish.

Towards sunset, the men who have been tapping rubber or working in their forest gardens walk down to the beach with clean clothes over their arms. They do not delay in the water, for the mosquitoes are becoming too numerous for bathing to be enjoyable unless one's whole body is kept under water.

There are no mosquitoes when the sun is shining, and by day the beach is a favourite haunt of the boys and girls—expert swimmers without exception, though they usually keep to the clear, shallow water where there is no danger of being bitten by the piranha. In the shallows the only dangers are the tawny sting-rays upon which the unwary may tread and get a vicious jab from a poisonous spur.

Chief among the boys is Manuel, who loves to come racing down the path from the village and hit the water like an arrow, making barely a splash. Then for a change, he will take a running leap, somersault and plunge into the water.

Where the beach ends, a pile of huge boulders overshadows the water, robbing it of that transparent freshness that bathers find so enticing on a hot day. By the stones, the river runs deeper. There is no DANGEROUS FOR BATHING notice, but none of the grown-ups ever bathe there, and from time to time, the youngsters are warned to keep to the beach and shallow water. Pedro the fisherman, who is headman of the village, has heard strange gurgles and splashes at night. Ducks disappear without trace. Nobody has solved the mystery of a missing dog.

Now Manuel is not the kind to be easily scared or put off. He found high diving from the boulders far more exciting than any running leap from sand. He dived and somersaulted so often that warnings became futile. The killer piranha fish only attack where there is bleeding, he reasoned. And opening his eyes under water, he could see no trace of them. So he began to regard as chicken the other boys who would not join him.

Then one day, when Manuel dived, he found himself up against something long, smooth and supple—something alive! And before he could surface, something covered his face, and things like knives cut into his cheeks. There can be no describing his feeling as it flashed upon him that an anaconda was getting him—no, had got him! At any moment he expected to feel the serpent's coils fasten round his body. There, in the depths of the river there could be no escape.

In his terror he prayed, "God help me!" and tore at the clammy mask on his face. To his unspeakable relief, it came away, and with his face stinging and streaming with blood he shot to the surface and scrambled ashore.

It was headman Pedro who offered an explanation to the awed villagers. "These serpents, after getting their teeth into anything, have to get their tails anchored to something solid before they can begin to crush.

The one which got our Manuel must have missed the submerged boulder at which it aimed its tail. That gave the boy his chance and he got away, thanks be to God."

Manuel's cheeks will always bear the marks of the river serpent's teeth but he has learned his lesson. He is taking no more risks. And as he tells his story and shows his scars, he is helping others not to make the same kind of mistake.

3

TREE-FROG'S NEST

I was in the forest with some of the Indians. Reaching a creek, we decided to rest for a while. The Indians took out their gourd bowls and had a hasty meal of farina and water, while I looked round for a place where the water ran clearest. On a sandy beach where the water was both shallow and clear, someone had walled-off a small, round pool, using sand from the river bed.

"Wild Indians!" I said to myself, "and they won't drink any old stuff either. How clever to think of filtering their drinking water through that wall of sand!" And taking out my collapsible aluminium cup I had a good drink of water from the inside of that pool.

When I rejoined my guides I told them of my discovery and my guess that wild Indians had passed that way.

"Wild Indians?" they laughed. "Indians don't make pools like that. That is the work of Koo-pok-koo-pok."

I knew that word. It was their name for a tree-frog. Was that pool a frog's nest? Yes, sure enough, nestling in a quiet corner was a cluster of frog-spawn! Koo-pok-koo-pok lives in the trees, the Indians explained, and only comes down to make her nest in the water. After laying her eggs she climbs back into the trees and forgets them. I did not really mind the laugh being on me, for I am always learning, and some of the most important lessons in life don't come from text-books.

A few days later, things began to happen in that pool my aluminium cup had disturbed for a moment. What should appear but a tadpole, and scores like him, wriggling up and down as tadpoles have always done. None of them were a bit concerned about all the splashing, gurgling and snapping going on just over the low wall of sand.

But as he grew arms and legs, the tadpole found that wall a bit of a nuisance. Which ever way he wanted to go, there it was right in front of him and confining his aquabatics to a space not much bigger than a pancake.

Then one day, he found himself amphibious, able to leave the water, climb the wall and see the world outside. There was no glimmer of appreciation in his eyes as they saw the forest beyond, the birds and butter-flies, and the little fish with their silvery scales lazing about in the water below. There was no flash of under-standing as big fish came dashing by and the little ones streaked for shelter among the stones or in the shallows where their enemy could not get at them. It did not dawn on him that there were jaws there which could have swallowed frog-spawn by the barrel had it not been for that little wall which had protected him until he could fend for himself. Frog minds could not be expected to reason things out, that walls don't just happen, that somebody has to build and that, somewhere, somebody has to plan.

As for our former tadpole, he just sat there sunning himself and seeing nothing but the tiny insects he somehow knew were there to be jumped for and devoured. Not a glimmer of wonder in his bulging eyes, not a spark of gratitude in his cold, unfeeling heart as he hopped away towards the bushes and trees destined to be his home for the rest of his life. But one day he will be down by the creek again, helping his mate build the very same kind of wall his unknown parents once built for him. He never saw other frogs at work, but, when his turn comes, he will not hesitate. He will make no mistakes. The wall he makes will be just right in size and shape, in just the right place and at just the right time.

How does he do so well at a job he never learned? Instinct, we say, or Nature!

The tadpole's protection came from a wee wall of sand. When God wants to illustrate His care for us, He takes us to something more solid.

"As the MOUNTAINS are round about Jerusalem, so the Lord is round about His people, from henceforth even for ever."

Psalm 125:2

4

WASTED YEARS OF THE TORTOISE

I've been reading about the Royal Tongan Tortoise which in 1773 was presented by Captain Cook to the King of Tonga, and was still living on May 19, 1966!

It set me thinking about the Brazilian tortoise our hunter brought in for dinner. A tortoise gets tough before he is out of his teens, and by the time he has made his first half-century his meat is really hard. You need a sharp hatchet, a strong arm and a hard heart to prepare him for the pot. Then with salt, pepper and onions, plus the milk from, say, 2 lbs. of grated Brazil nuts, you have a delicious meal. When the liver is fried separately, its taste resembles that of grilled mushrooms. And when the tortoise is a female, and there are eggs to fry along with the liver, the meal is better still.

In the Old Testament, the tortoise and his kind are rated as unclean and forbidden. He was never meant to be eaten. With his flat, armour plate below, and the rounded, stream-lined dome above, he had little to fear. Rain cannot wet him or hornets sting him. He is safe from both hawks and dogs. He cannot be crushed by either the peccary's hammer hooves or the anaconda's coils. The fierce piranha fish may snap off a leg as he swims across a river, but such a wound is never fatal. And after being once bitten, he is more than twice shy.

It isn't just the defensive armour which helps him. Disposition helps his mind as the shell protects his body. He is quiet and easy going. He makes no enemies, never hurries or worries. He makes himself at home anywhere, on land or in the water, in forest, field or back garden, provided it is not too cold. He never works, for he makes neither burrow nor nest. He is never bothered with a family. Not that he doesn't mate. The female lays one egg here and another egg there and leaves the rest to Nature. From the very first day after hatching out, the youngsters have to fend for themselves. The tortoise could not care less about anything or anybody—except when a hunter has him tied up and he feels that his own precious life is in danger. Then he will really work to free himself.

But in spite of armour-plate, slow motion and living as a palace pet for nearly 200 years, the Royal Tongan Tortoise died on May 19, 1966. And what did he have to show for having lived so long? Just nothing!

What a picture of so many humans! We cannot hope to stay in the world as long as the Royal Tongan Tortoise, but God does give to most of us a full seventy

years of opportunity, not just to live and die, but to do something really worth while in a world full of human need. He means us to enjoy life to the full by living it for Him and with Him.

Jesus said: "He that loveth his life shall lose it but whosoever shall lose his life for My sake, the same shall find it."

I once took an Indian to town to spend some money he had earned. Wanting to help him with the buying, I was shocked when he told me that he had already lost all his money. Then, seeing the effect of what he had said, he went on, "But look what I have found." And he proudly displayed the new clothes, the knife, mirror and other things he had bought.

There are no commercial terms in his language, no words for earning and spending, buying and selling, so he was adapting. He had not lost his money. He had spent it. And in spending it he had found something of far more practical value than his coins and banknotes.

And so to lose a life for Jesus is to spend it with Him and for Him. How can young people do that? First of all by making up your minds that whatever others may or may not be, you are going to be a committed Christian and live your life not just for yourself but for the Lord Jesus who died to make you His own.

5

SQUIRREL AND THE SNAKE

If "every picture tells a story", so does every snake skin we see being stretched in its frame of split bamboo for drying in the sun. The one I found my hunter friend at work on was twelve feet long. He was only too ready to tell me the story.

He had made no noise as he trod the forest's carpet of dead leaves, sodden and smelly after weeks of rain. Game was elusive, but he figured that in the nut grove there might be something to kill and take home to his hungry family. Scattered around like so many rusty cannon balls were Brazil nuts, still intact in their heavy outer casing. The hunter walked cautiously, for nuts were still falling with a dull thud and he knew that a direct hit could crack a man's skull.

A hundred yards ahead, an agouti* was quietly, steadily working on one of the nuts. Brazil nuts are hard and his teeth had been at work since the first light of day. An agouti is a Brazilian ground squirrel, the size of a rabbit and in colour ginger-red. Without any tail he has little of the glamour of his bushy-tailed relative frolicking in the branches above his head. However, he is very cute to watch as he squats on his haunches and nibbles the food he holds in his short paws.

*Agouti is the Indian name, pronounced 'a good tea'

After a time of patient, industrious nibbling, the agouti of our story paused in his work and began to look around. Right then, something caught his eye, something which must have given him a jolt, for he at once dropped the nut on which he was working and began running round. Deeply agitated, he lost all interest in what he had been doing—his food, his work, his customary caution, indeed, in everything but the silly little dance he was doing on that stage of wet leaves.

He scurried to and fro, seemingly in a dreadful hurry, but getting nowhere. He would go away, but he always came back, his strange circuit getting smaller and smaller, and nearer and nearer the spot where that mysterious something had first caught his eye.

Hearing the pitter-patter of tiny feet, the approaching hunter crept forward and saw what the agouti was doing. "That animal is surely bewitched," he said to himself, and began to look around to see what was holding it in so strange yet so powerful a charm.

Yes, there, sure enough, motionless as a tree trunk and with green eyes unblinking, waited anaconda, the boa constrictor, all ready to catch, to crush and to kill! Her victims rarely get away. Even before her teeth bite into the neck, they are doomed. It is enough that she catches their eye.

But this time, just as her head was poised to strike and write *finis* to the agouti's career, the hunter fired.

"And what happened to the agouti?" I asked, as I admired the fine skin and heard his story. "Did you kill him too?"

"No," came the reply. "I let him go."

I found myself feeling glad, relieved that the little fellow should have been given another chance. I was thinking about young Christians at home—and older ones too—who go the same way as the agouti. Busily and happily engaged in Christian service—Sunday

School, Christian Endeavour, Youth for Christ, Crusaders and Covenanters—with a practical interest in overseas missions and Bible School training, they suddenly see something or hear something which sweeps them off their feet. They drop everything and lose all interest.

This is nothing new and not at all peculiar to this day and age. "O foolish Galatians, who hath bewitched you?" cried the Apostle Paul.

His lament was that they had taken their eyes from Jesus and left themselves easy victims when the serpent of error raised its head to strike.

It was good for the agouti that at his zero hour there was someone at hand who was more than a match for the serpent and all its wiles. If ever we find ourselves being caught, we may be sure that the Lord Jesus will be a very present help in our trouble, if we will but call upon Him.

6

TAMING THE PECCARY

It is surprising that in these vast forests there should be no really *big* game, no lions, tigers, elephants, hippos or rhinos. As far as individual animals go, the striped jaguar is king of all the South American beasts.

However, the real terrors of these jungles are the peccary, or wild hogs. They are very different from domestic pigs. For one thing, they have no tails! In colour, they are black, hairy and with bristles running down their spines. They rove the forest in herds, and they are vicious, clicking their teeth and grinding their long, sharp tusks. In the ordinary way, nothing can stand up to them. Small animals get trampled under-foot. Snakes don't often get a chance to bite—and when they do, it seems that their poison has no effect. Even the jaguar has to be careful how he sets about getting a dinner of wild pig. He dare not risk a frontal attack, but must pounce on a straggler, and, after making a quick kill, be ready to move out of the way until the angry, tusk-grinding pack has moved on.

When hunters are armed with repeating rifles and work together, they can usually kill a big number and send the herd away in confusion. But not always. It depends on how the hoary old boar leading the pack reacts to the shooting, and whether he snorts a retreat or a charge! Most of my hunter friends can tell of occasions when, after emptying the magazine, they have had to shin up the nearest tree for safety.

One Indian hunter I know, over-confident in the possession of a shot-gun, delayed just a little too long and was knocked to the ground and badly gored. He barely managed to reach a tree in time to save himself from being trampled to death. His legs will always bear the marks of those teeth and tusks.

One day a big herd had been ravaging the forest gardens of maize and manioc, and the Indians went all-out for revenge. Some of them boasted old shot-guns but had few bullets. Those who had arrows carried short clubs too, not wanting to leave themselves defence-less when the last arrow had been shot.

The herd was bigger and tougher than usual and, instead of being routed by the shooting, they charged! One savage creature snapped his teeth right through the leading Indian's hand, although he did manage to stun it with his club. As the hunters trooped into the village with their numerous victims, the women did a burst of wailing in sympathy for the wounded man and also for the gored dogs limping home with drooping tails.

Late that night Donna Eva was called in to ease the Indian's pain. The medicine-man had been along to kipper the wound with tobacco smoke, but this was a case for cleaning out, not covering up, and for a shot of penicillin and careful treatment over many days.

Meanwhile, village life was enlivened by the squeak-ing and grunting of two tiny, baby peccaries the hunters had brought home. The women fed them. The children played with them as if they were puppies or kittens.

One morning when I had been to see the injured man, a little piglet followed me home. Out of the lodge, across the village square, right into our house as if he had known me all his life! I had quite a job to avoid treading on him, for he kept right under my feet. He would eat out of my hand and, wherever I went, was never more than a few inches from my heels.

After a while, a wee Red Indian boy came along to claim his pet. He looked so cute with his copper-coloured skin, jet-black hair and eyes brimful of sparkle. It was hard to believe that such lovable boys could ever grow up to be the fearsome, pitiless killers who have terrorized the River X for so long!

I did not say so, but I was thinking the boy would not have an easy task in getting his pet away from me and our nice clean house. But it was the quickest, easiest thing in the world! All the boy did was to get his feet in between the piglet's snout and my heels! In one moment, it left off following me and followed him, out of the house and into the village. And, believe me, could a forest peccary have suddenly cut in between the little boy's feet and the little pig's trotters, it would have been back in the jungle in no time, and just one more in a big, wild, vicious herd.

How do Indians tame peccary? It's easy. They just make the most of that instinct to follow the feet which are nearest. The feet which guide the trotters will decide the future of the tusks.

And who will say that young humans don't have a "follow-instinct" too, whether they be redskin or paleface?

That is why we missionaries are here. We want our feet to be worth following, as we, for our part, seek to follow the One who said, "I am the Way".

7

THE ANTEATER

One of the Indians has a wonderful pet. Only a toddler as yet, it is no bigger than a dog, although its head is already a foot long, all snout, narrow and tapering like a parsnip. Donna Eva and the children got a fright when it put out its tongue at them. They thought a snake was coming out of its mouth! Ears and eyes are tiny. The front legs are longer and stronger than the back ones and all four are armed with great claws. The body is covered with long, coarse hair, black and grey. But queerest of all is the flat, bushy tail, big enough to use as an umbrella when it rains and as a blanket at night. When he grows up, he will be a Great Anteater, or Ant-bear.

True to his name, he really eats ants and, as far as I can see, he will eat nothing else. In the Zoo, he gives his keeper a hard time to keep him fed. For the Indian, feeding his pet is no problem at all, for there are ant-hills all over the place in these parts. The anteater's preference is for white ants, or termites.

Termites are horrible little creatures which work underground and keep us on the alert lest they should

gnaw into our boxes, books and furniture, and even the wooden framework of the house we live in. Were it not for the problems in looking after such a pet and taking him around with us on our travels, I should be tempted to make an offer for that anteater. How convenient to have him around the house, relieving me of all concern for our wooden possessions.

The anteater's one aim in life seems to be to rid the earth of termites. His strong, hooked arms were built for breaking into ant-hills. The tapered snout and snake-like tongue are his equipment for rooting out the ants from their clay strongholds. Angry insects swarm on to the invading tongue as it licks around, thinking no doubt to sting it into retreat. Retreat it does, but only into its mouth, and with it, all the clinging ants as well.

Around he goes, from ant-hill to ant-hill, breaking them open, mopping up their occupants and generally doing a good job. It is a hopeless task, though, for ant-hills are so many and anteaters so few. And instead of appreciating the good work he is doing, the Indians are all too ready to kill and eat him. How easy it would be for the anteater to get discouraged, to give up his mission and go in for eating bananas or even wild fruits. But he never runs away, either from his work or from his enemies.

Whenever he is attacked, he always stands firm, Rearing himself on his hind legs, and raising that flag of a tail, he opens wide his arms and makes his claws stick out like the knives in Boadicea's chariot wheels. Even the jaguar will not risk a frontal attack. If he cannot take him by surprise and get him from behind, he will leave him alone, for he knows that once that anteater's hooked arms get a hold, they will never let go, not even in death.

The Indians have learned a lot from the animals who

share their jungle empire, mostly along the lines of camouflage and being wily, tough and relentless. It is from the anteater that they have learned the value of standing firm. Indian boys never run away in a fight, even though they cannot hope to win. They just stand their ground, giving and taking until licked.

The anteater's tenacity is a lesson to Donna Eva and me as we seek to win these Indians for Jesus. Ant-hills of superstition we have demolished by the score, but still they appear. The tribe, instead of joining us for a Christian Christmas, staged a week's commemoration of the time when some painted women turned themselves into fish! And how many ant-hills of cruelty have we not attacked! Yet most Indians delight to kill and are amused at the sufferings of others. In their recent feast, scores of big turtles were roasted alive after a hole had been hammered in each shell. Other ant-hills still persisting are those of indifference and callousness.

We carry on, trying to be kind among the cruel, loving the unloved, the unloving and the ungrateful, and seeking to keep clean among the dirty in body, home and mind.

8

THE BOA TURNS TO SOAP

We are in town for a few weeks. We came down the River X in a trader's launch. The days were long, our seats were hard and whenever the owner called a halt for trading, the sand flies swarmed on board and piled on the agony until we got going again and the wind could blow them away.

There was more foam on the water than usual, and James mistook it for soap suds. I had to explain the difference between soap suds and the kind of foam we see on our River X. Foam may be just air bubbles caused when water runs up against rocks, trees, or the prow of a boat. Where there are rapids or falls the whole river may become a seething mass of foam. Eddies and whirlpools make foam too—not very white, for they have a way of churning all kinds of impurities out of the water. I suggested that the foam might be coming from Indian fish poison. I told him how all the men in a village will carry a heavy sheaf of poison vines to the water and hammer them to pulp with their clubs. In a few minutes the water is covered by a mass of foam which poisons the water and soon has the poor fish gasping for breath, their tummies turned upwards and providing the Indians with easy targets for their arrows.

Then I remember another story of foam on the water.

There was once a pig—just an ordinary pig wallowing in the mud by the riverside. But his grunts of contentment suddenly became squeals of fright as he felt himself being hugged by a boa constrictor. Up in the village, a man heard the squealing and, guessing what was happening, picked up his gun and raced down the path to the river. Though too late to save the pig, he killed the boa and soon had it unwound from the pig and rewound on a long pole for carrying to the village.

Everybody crowded round to watch as he first removed the valuable skin and then sliced the flesh into steaks. That man knew that the boa was as fat as it was long. For every inch of her eight feet of life she had been piling up the fat as she preyed—first of all on frogs, rats and lizards, and then as she grew longer and stronger, on larger animals. And now the

28

man was going to fry her steaks for the fat they would yield.

What would he do with so much boa fat? People in the interior of Brazil may live right off the beaten track and so have to be as independent as they possibly can in the matter of supplies. They may have to make their own lamp oil from oil-yielding wild fruits. They need to know how to make their own soap too. And it was with the help of a tin of caustic soda that our friend was going to turn the boa fat into soap.

That was the end of the mighty boa constrictor. Nothing but soap suds to show for a whole lifetime! And as the river carried those suds away, nobody gave them so little as a look.

9

PLAYING 'POSSUM

We are still away from the Indians and living in our chalet home on the River X. The house has been empty for more than a year and, in our absence, the rats have taken possession. Indeed, the whole town is plagued with them. Our neighbour, who bakes to sell from door to door, has a sack of flour from which she just could not keep the rats away, until she and her husband decided to take the flour to bed with them and give it the protection of their mosquito net!

Another neighbour did not take proper care of his artificial teeth and when he awoke one morning, he found them gone from his bedside table. He spent the whole day on the roof of his home, looking between the tiles and the rafters where rats have their hideout during daylight hours. He only got them back after several weeks when the people next-door-but-one had had their roof repaired and the denture was found.

In the chalet, young Jim has taken to baiting our rat-traps instead of his fish hooks. One night, when he went to our outside bathroom, he saw a rat as big as a cat, not an ordinary rat, for apart from its great size, its hair was longer and its movement slower. It was an opossum.

Like the kangaroo, the female has a pouch in which to carry her babies, and when these get too big for the pouch and yet are still too small to fend for themselves, they cling to their mother's fur coat wherever they can get a hold.

The opossum did not run away when discovered, so

out of pity we took no action against him. However, when next night we saw him there again, we suspected that he was making our bathroom his headquarters for raids on our neighbours' chickens. Jim aimed a blow at him with an Indian club but being rather long, the descending club hit the low roof and broke a tile instead of the opossum's head. The next time we saw him was on top of a fence. Clearly loitering with intent to commit a felony, as the police would say, we decided that the opossum had to die. A single shot from a gun sent him toppling to earth like a stone. Jim was for climbing the fence right away and hauling out the prize from the clump of foliage into which he had fallen, but, opossums being smelly things, I told him to leave it until morning.

But when morning came, there wasn't a trace of the "dead" opossum. He can cleverly pretend to be dead where there is a chance of saving his life, and with us his ruse worked all too well and he made a clean getaway.

"Playing 'possum" is something we humans can do too. If it means an easy way out of a difficulty, we can feign to be dead or sick or pretend not to know something when all the time we do. There are a number of Bible stories of people who could play 'possum when it suited their interests, pretending to be sick or ignorant of what they knew to be true. There was St. Peter, for instance, who lay very low when a girl challenged him about knowing Jesus. At that fireside he looked more like a dead worldling than a live disciple of Jesus Christ.

10

DON'T BE AN ARMADILLO

This is the rainy season and the River X is in flood. With many of the rapids now under water, we find it more convenient than in the dry season for getting around in our little boat and visiting the settlers who have their homes on the river banks.

Below the very last rapid and for the nearly two hundred miles before the River X flows into the Amazon, is a long, clear stretch of water which is navigable to big river steamers. In those waters are creatures which fight shy of rapids and rough waters, for they are never encountered in the upper reaches of the river. Such are the dophins (regarded by the natives as being enchanted), the giant cow-fish, and the famous tartarugas. These are turtles which may weigh as much as one hundred pounds and are in great demand for the tables of the monied class, as the flesh is considered to be a greater delicacy than that of turkeys.

It is not surprising, therefore, that as we travelled through those waters, our conversation should be of dolphins and fresh-water turtles.

In the midst of our talking we had to call at one of the riverside homes. As we moored our boat the women of the household were at work on a big pile of fresh meat. There, sure enough, a few yards away, was a real whopper of a yellow, horny shell.

"Stay for a meal," the good folks invited. We did.

"Well," said Donna Eva as the meal over, we proceeded on our way, "If that was the wonderful tartaruga turtle, I just cannot understand people being so crazy about it."

"Tartaruga?" I exclaimed. "Who said that was tartaruga? Do you think that everything in a big shell is turtle? That wasn't tartaruga at all, but an armadillo!"

The expression on Donna Eva's face was a mixture of dismay and disgust, for she had never eaten armadillo before.

The Indians tell us that he is the most ancient of all animals. He began life, so they say, up in Heaven, but, being a great burrower from the beginning, he one day burrowed right through the floor of Heaven and fell down to Earth!

Digging is the armadillo's favourite means of defence, even though Nature has given him a coat of armour which covers him from nose to tail. At the slightest alarm he begins to dig himself in, and down into the earth he goes with amazing speed. Scratching away with his front legs, he uses his back ones to hurl the dirt clear. Woe betide the hunting dog who gets caught in the back-fire from that furious digging!

Fancy living in this vast, wonderful forest, yet only venturing out under cover of darkness. Fancy having such a coat of armour and yet not using it except as protection against falls of earth and sand as he digs on and on, to comfort and safety. Why, with such equipment, the armadillo could laugh at cold and rain, thorn and thicket, snake and hawk, hornet and nettle, and make life one long thrill!

There is a streak in his inside make-up as yellow as his armour plate. The armadillo is just plain scared of everything and everybody!

As regards diet, he lives on grubs, earth worms and—

like the anteater—termites. Of course, the latter has much the harder time with no armour to protect him.

How I wish I could get the two of them together. If only I could encourage the armadillo to face the light of day, to take a stand like the anteater or, better still, to take a stand with him. How cheered the old termite fighter would be to have an ally at his side. If only they would pool their resources. But our two friends are only animals. They haven't the sense to get together and work together. The sad thing is when we humans try to imitate them.

If there are tough Christians who sing "Stand up, stand up for Jesus" and do it, there are also the other kind, armadillo Christians, armchair ones, whose concern seems to be to keep as safe and comfortable as possible. To say that they are just cautious, or tactful, in their witness, is much too charitable. I know what kind of Christians we need to be.

11

SLOW AS A SLOTH

Hanging head downwards from a rafter! My first impression was of an ageing monkey, for its dark brown hair was greying, fast asleep. It was a sloth. I was glad to see him, for he is a rare sight, even in the Brazilian forest.

Fossils show that the sloth family was once numerous, with some members as big as elephants. But Providence seems to have fashioned them all on the basis of one ounce of brain to each ton of brawn, which wasn't enough to ensure survival in a competitive world. Perhaps before very long even this Brazilian variety will become extinct too, with nobody at all to lament its passing.

I had no difficulty in getting a photograph, for as regards movement, the sloth is in the tortoise class. And in a flat race, the tortoise would win easily, for to get along at all, the sloth needs to be up in a tree. He was born in a tree, he lives in a tree and in the ordinary way he will die in a tree, though it would be exaggerating to add "and all in the same tree". On the ground, or in the water, it is pitiful to see him, for instead of having hands and feet, he is fitted with big claws which can only be used for hanging on to branches. He cannot walk, stand or even sit. He lives hanging on, and upside down he goes, all the way from his cradle to his grave.

He was quite unmoved by my stroking and efforts to show myself friendly. I fancy he would have been just as indifferent to pokes or threats. Though neither hungry nor tied up, he just surveyed me sadly through dull, watery eyes.

"Poor you!" I muttered, as I turned away. "Whoever would want to be a sloth. And yet you must be here for some purpose."

Then I remembered a verse in my Bible: "Not slothful in business." From now onwards I shall want to read, "Not sloth-like."

Let me complete that verse from the Bible: "Not slothful in business, fervent in spirit, serving the Lord." That is being something more than just a human being and not an animal. It means being a Christian, and for that, I'm gladdest of all, for the Lord gives faith and hope, joy and peace, light and love.

12

GOAT-SUCKER'S BAD NAME

There is never any knowing what Jim will bring home when he goes off with the Indians. He may come in asking for an empty matchbox in which to house a pet frog. Or he may be wanting a piece of string with which to harness a wee trailer to a midget tortoise, or a gondola to some queer flying insect.

The other day his trophy was a baby bird, the most unattractive thing imaginable. It had no feathers at all and the only movement made was with its big mouth which gaped hungrily all the time. Jim's first concern was to give it something to eat. He tried it with rice, cooked and raw. He tried it with farina meal, wet and dry. But all to no avail.

It was then that I tried to help. "First of all," I suggested, "we must find out what kind of a bird it is. If it is a hawk, it will need meat, if a gull or heron we must give it fish. If it belongs to the swallow family, we must try it with insects."

When we asked the Indians, we were told that the bird was a porro-pot, which of course left us none the wiser. Then I went to our home-made dictionary of the Indian language. Over the years we have never heard a new word without writing it down. Well, that dictionary gave us porro-pot's Brazilian equivalent. The rest was easy. Turning up the big Brazilian-English dictionary I discovered that porro-pot is Indian for bacurau which in turn has three names in English—nightjar, night-hawk and goat-sucker.

Nothing much to look at, the grown bird is quite drab in this land of so many gaudy feathers. It delights to sit on a patch of bare ground on a moonlight night. Sometimes it gives the impression of not being able to fly properly or that it has a damaged wing, half-flying half-jumping in a way that tempts you to give chase. It is usually the female bird that does this, endeavouring to lead unwelcome intruders away from her nest.

We mixed some powdered milk and administered it in a small teaspoon. The experiment was not a success. Indeed, it was fatal. The poor bird just gave one long gurgle and died. Milk was clearly NOT its proper food, goat-sucker or no.

Now had there been time for me to check up the facts, I would have learned that the name goat-sucker comes from the now exploded tradition that these birds pester mother goats in order to steal their milk. What they are really doing is mopping up the flies, gnats, mosquitoes and other insect pests which are all too ready to torment defenceless animals. In doing their best to help the goats, the poor birds got themselves a bad name, which got first of all into people's minds and then into their books.

I was once visiting a colony of leprosy sufferers near the mouth of the Amazon, and among them I met several who had recently arrived there from the River X. They were all feeling the separation from home and loved ones as well as the terrible depression which follows the doctor's diagnosis of leprosy. Some of them were Christian believers and the fact that others were not made no difference to the distribution of gifts of money I was able to make. Before coming away I prayed with them, the most and the best I could do for them in their plight.

When the husband of one of the sufferers who was not a Christian heard of what I had done he wrote to me. Not a Christian himself, he complained that I was trying to make a Christian of his wife by helping her. The letter ended with a demand that I should make no further visits and no further gifts without his permission.

There is no need for a Christian to be a foreign missionary to know how easily we can be misunderstood. Just take a stand for Jesus Christ and watch it happen, whether at school, or place of employment, or in one's own home. The crowd is not always right. Jesus IS always right and nobody ever yet followed Him all the way and regretted it.

13

KILLER FISH FOR SUPPER

On our river journeys we always get very hungry, so as they paddle our boat the Indians are on the alert for fish and game. One day, as the overhead sun as well as our hungry tummies suggested a halt for something to eat, we were all glad to spot some beautiful, silver fish which were jumping up to snap at leaves hanging low over the water. Very quietly, one of the Indians picked up his bow and arrows. Up to the surface came a fish and in the split second during which it was air-borne, the bow-string twanged. It was a wonderful shot, for the arrow transfixed the fish and turned it over on its side.

Next job was to take it from the water, but as the current was fairly strong, arrow and fish were being carried downstream. Before we could overtake the still struggling fish, the arrow gave a sudden jump and when, moments later, we took it from the water, all that remained of our fish was the head! The killer fish were on the war-path and our dinner was gone!

One of our men strode off into the forest with his gun and returned to camp with a bird little bigger than a starling.

Using pieces of the bird for bait, in a few minutes the good man had caught enough killer fish (piranhas) for dinner and supper too, because of all Brazilian fish, piranhas are just about the easiest to catch. They dash madly at any kind of bleeding bait. The only problem is to get them unhooked without getting a finger snapped off!

Some are as grey as lead, some as gay as goldfish. Some are fifteen inches long, others stop growing at six inches. But all are killers, blood-hungry killers. Their teeth are like newly sharpened rip saws, and when they close they click. They hunt in packs like wolves, but keep to deep water except when they surface at the noise of a splash or at the scent of blood.

If one has a cut or open sore, it is dangerous to bathe in our beautiful River X.

Animals need the river as much as we do. When hunted they always make for the water in the hope of putting the hunter or his dogs off the scent. But should the piranhas be there, attracted by the bleeding, flesh can be stripped from bone in a few seconds and a living body reduced to a skeleton.

As we watched the fish being prepared for the pot, Donna Eva remarked that she is not surprised that some writers refer to our rain forests, with their killer-fish and jaguars, anacondas and crocodiles, as "Green Hell".

It was not long before we were enjoying our meal of cooked piranha, stripping fish from bone with that enthusiasm born of a good appetite.

"No problem, these killer fish," I said to Donna Eva, my mouth more full than perhaps it ought to have been. "Their human victims are few, for they are easily avoided and readily caught. There is nothing we need do about them but keep out of their way. But human beings are different. They can be forgiven, converted, changed, saved!"

And that is our mission in life. In a modern world, haunted and torn by killer-things, inspired by killer-thinking, fed and fanned by killer books and even toys, we know that Jesus alone can give LIFE.

"The Son of man is not come to destroy men's lives, but to save them."   (Luke 9:56)

14

BLUE BUTTERFLY?

I have seen the biggest, most beautiful butterfly of a lifetime! It had a wing span of six inches and, although brown on the underside, the top of its wings was a dazzling blue which sparkled in the morning sunlight. Knowing what a marvellous curio such a prize would make, I dropped the tools with which I was working and gave chase, hoping it would alight on one of our coffee bushes which were in full blossom. However, it flew on, right over the garden fence and into the forest beyond.

Some days after the blue butterfly escaped me, I noticed a tiny caterpillar on our jasmine tree. There is nothing very attractive about its gnarled, crooked trunk and branches, but the leaves are a luscious green all the year round and the flowers are as white as Easter lilies and so fragrant that the scent carries more than fifty yards. Flowers are rare on the River X and our jasmine tree can be like a breath of paradise in a dreary world of mud and mosquitoes. We love it. As I examined the caterpillar, I saw it was not alone. There were lots of them, tiny creatures decked in black velvet jerseys with gold stripes and lying motionless on the underside of the branches.

The idea came to me that the big blue butterfly might have laid its eggs there while passing through our garden. What matter that the caterpillars should be black and gold and the parent blue and brown? The caterpillar need bear no resemblance to the butterfly into which—one day—it will be transformed.

So the caterpillars were allowed to stay, even when they began to rear their heads and jab at the leaves like hungry woodpeckers. They simply gorged themselves and grew at the rate of nearly an inch a day. By the end of the week they were six inches long and almost an inch in diameter. If I had never seen so big a butterfly, I was now seeing the biggest caterpillars too.

"Who would have thought it?" I said to myself as our once lovely tree was stripped of its leaves and the ground below it became littered with stalks and droppings. "To think that those cute, gay, innocent-looking little fellows should grow up into such terrors!"

One morning the children came in to tell me that all my pet caterpillars, as they called them, were going away. I went into the garden and found the jasmine tree as bare of caterpillars as it was of leaves. Some were hurrying down the trunk, others were hunching themselves along the ground in the direction of the fence. Some had already climbed the fence and were arching their heads as if looking for other jasmine trees to conquer.

Finding an old iron pot, I lined it with leaves and went round collecting as many caterpillars as I could, picking them up between two sticks, placing them in the nest and covering the pot with a roofing tile. When the children asked me what I was doing, I told them how we were going to have a wonderful object lesson of how God can change bad things and make them good, and how He changes bad people too.

"We'll look at them every day," I said. "One day the nasty things are going to be changed into wonderful butterflies and then they will flit around in the sunlight like the bees and humming-birds."

Next day the caterpillars were dull and listless. Their once gay jerseys were losing their shine. Their appetites had gone too, for not a single leaf had been nibbled, but they still reared their heads angrily when lightly touched with a stick.

A few days later, they had become chrysalides. The caterpillar skins and legs were dry and shrivelled and had been cast aside like old clothes. Jim picked them up and handled the black chrystalides without fear.

Each day we peeped into that iron pot, all eager to be on the spot when the great change should take place.

At last it happened. The hard black shells split from end to end. There was movement inside. Would the first glimpse of wing be blue or brown?

It was neither. Instead of the exquisite blue we expected to see, there emerged the ugliest, most horrid, loathsome moths I have ever seen! The children were disgusted.

"Witch-moth!" cried Jim's Brazilian playmate.

Even when they emerged from their coffin-like shells, the creatures made no effort to fly away. To the witch-moth, the brightness of the sunshine, the fragrance of flowers, the company of honey-bees and humming-birds mean nothing at all. It was not until after sunset that they showed signs of movement and we watched them unfold their wings and flutter clumsily away into the darkness.

This had been an object lesson very different from what I expected. Butterflies and moths, there is always an opposite. That is the lesson for us to learn. There is always an opposite.

There is nothing at all a caterpillar can do about its future state. It either becomes a butterfly or a moth, according to its kind. It cannot choose between light and darkness. We can. We can be good or bad. We can obey God or disobey Him. We can be saved or lost. And it is for us to choose.

15

TWO BIRDS IN ONE

Donna Eva stood by an open window, looking up into the sky and shading her eyes from the glare.

"Look at those birds," she said, "Oh, to be able to fly so high where there's a cool wind and the air is so fresh and untainted by the things of earth!"

The birds certainly made a fine sight. There were perhaps a dozen of them, gliding majestically at a great height, with only the occasional flip of a wing to show that they were birds and not machines.

"You've seen them many a time on the fence at the foot of our backyard. They're vultures!"

Donna Eva did not try to hide her surprise. She knew the vulture well enough. There is no mistaking him, with his dull, black feathers, his bald pate and hooked beak. His favourite perch is the branch of a lofty tree whence his eye can cover a wide area. He may often be seen on a fence or roof overlooking a kitchen door. There he will sit for hours on end, waiting for scraps of offal or garbage. He has no appetite for the daintier scraps thrown out to the sparrows and starlings. He is a scavenger, only wanting that which is smelly and in decomposition.

He has a clumsy, lurching way of walking. His take-off from the ground is a real effort, with nothing graceful about it. As he moves from scrap to scrap, or fights for his share of the victim, he has a way of half-jumping, half-flying.

His sense of smell and sight is truly amazing. He is quick to see any sick or wounded animal likely to die, and the smell of death guides him unerringly through any covering of thicket or forest roof-top of foliage, no matter how dense these may be. With his sharp hooked bill and strong talons, his meal does not take him long. His companions are always so many and so hungry. There is rarely enough meat to go round.

After feeding, he makes for the river and spends some time splashing his great wings in the water and sunning himself on the shore or on a convenient branch of a tree. Then up he soars, to heights unreached by any other bird. If among the garbage he is loathsome, in the air he is superb!

He returns to earth after a while and then, blue skies, clean air, washing and sunning seemingly forgotten, he is back to his scavenging among the garbage and offal.

"How strange!" murmured Donna Eva. "What a queer mix-up of two natures in the one bird. How can he be so much at home in two such opposite spheres?

How can he fly so high, and then, so quickly afterwards, be ready to stoop so low?"

It is clear to me that there are two natures common to all men. If we are honest with ourselves we can recognize their presence in our own hearts. We can see them at work in our children. In young and old alike is the conflict between good and bad. Few will dare say that they are all good, yet none will denounce themselves as wholly bad. Who never wants to soar? But who never comes down to the level of the mean and unworthy?

God never meant us to live like vultures, up and down, now soaring, now stooping, now glorying, now grovelling. There is a way not only to get away from sin, but to keep away. St. Paul gives us the answer: "I thank God, through Jesus Christ our Lord."

16

THE ELECTRIC EEL

There are days in these rain forests when Donna Eva is unable to make the grade in the kitchen. It is not enough to be able to cook a meal. A really good cook must know how to catch something to cook!

That is how a friend of ours came to be wading in the river an hour before supper time. Mosquitoes were few so he was not wearing a shirt. Over his shoulder, a shot-gun hung by a leather strap. Over his arm was folded the fishing net he was all set for casting as he moved stealthily towards the spot where he calculated the fish might be. Suddenly, with a yell like someone mortally wounded, he went down like a shot, arms and legs flailing the water. His leg had brushed against an electric eel! Good for him that the water was shallow enough to lie there until the first effects of the shock had passed. Then, with all thoughts of kitchen and evening meal forgotten, he made for the house and his hammock, to seek relief from the aching leg.

I had often heard stories of electric-eels, but this was the first case personally known to me, and after seeing a victim, I became keener than ever to examine an aggressor.

The opportunity came one Sunday morning. Our morning service had been disappointing for all the boys were absent. Waking up very hungry, they decided to go fishing. They were not long away, and long before they came in sight, we all knew they were not coming empty-handed. When there is no kill, or when the catch is a small one, Indians are ashamed and try to sneak into the village without being seen. When the haul is a big one, they make a lot of noise. That Sunday, the shouting was so loud they might well have been bringing in a jaguar.

It was an electric eel, still very much alive, dragged along on the end of a rope-like creeper.

"Here you are, Orat," said one of the boys. "You often asked us to get one alive. Now you can take its picture."

It was a tricky operation getting that eel hung up to a beam in our kitchen but the boys were most careful to avoid contact. I noticed that the drag rope was quite dry. Experience has taught the Indians the ABC of insulation. After all, their ancestors knew all about shocks before ours did!

The eel was not a big one, just four feet long and as thick as a man's arm. The dark green body had no scales and there was a soft, rippling fin stretching along the underside from head to tail. The head was flat with a gaping mouth and the tiniest of eyes. The drag-rope had somehow been threaded through its gills.

I was looking at the wonderful creature which is dynamo, battery and discharge coil all combined. For the first time ever, there was electricity in our kitchen! Having read somewhere that the current produced is as much as 500 volts, I went for a voltmeter. Maybe I could get some kind of response on the dial.

"Don't touch it! It will knock you down!" yelled the Indians.

In due time the eel died and was cut down and handed back to the boys who, hungrier than ever, prepared for a feast. I watched very carefully as they did the cutting and slicing, but saw no clue as to the source of the creature's power.

Indians believe that they become like the things they eat. They eat the howling monkey to be resistant and tough, the jaguar to be fierce, the electric-eel to make their presence felt and feared. The stronger and wilder they can become, the better their chances of one day becoming a chief.

I suppose we have all met people who would make good Red Indians, and chiefs at that! They never saw an electric-eel, much less ate one. But they have a way of throwing their weight about in a way that hurts. Things they say, looks they give—words, looks, deeds can hurt just as much as live wires.

Wild, primitive people have their own ideals. The heroes of their legends were all fierce warriors with super-strength, magic weapons and a bent for killing. Now they are hearing of Someone who was different. Who like Jesus could say "All power is given unto Me, in heaven and in earth"? Yet, for all that power, He was so kind, so wonderful to know.

For instance, there was that poor woman we read about in the Gospels. Desperately ill for twelve years, all her money gone in doctors' bills, yet without relief.

48

Hearing of Jesus and His power, she crept forward in the crowd, reached out and touched the hem of His garment. She was not hurt, but healed.

The Indians often ask me why God made this and that. If I were to ask them why God made electric eels I think I know what many of them would answer: "To show us how to be!"

Everything must have been made for a purpose although very often we cannot understand what that purpose may be. I can think of at least one reason why God made electric-eels.

"To show us how NOT to be!"

17

PUTTING UP THE GREEN PARASOL

"Whatever makes you grow your cabbages and lettuces on those big tables?" asked our visitors. No wonder they were surprised. Just as ancient Babylon had its Hanging Gardens—whatever they were—here in interior Brazil we have our gardens on stilts!

This is because of the parasol-ants. The land is honeycombed with their burrows. If we made our kitchen garden at ground level, they could strip it in a single night. Parasol ants are so called because they are usually seen carrying pieces of fresh leaves like so many green sun-shades.

The Bible says: "The ants are a people not strong yet they prepare their meat in the summer" (Proverbs 30:25). "Go to the ant thou sluggard, consider her ways and be wise" (Proverbs 6:6).

Here we have stood amazed at their industry, at the way they can work round the clock to lay up leaves in their underground storehouses. They never seem to get discouraged, not even when the wind gets into their parasols and bowls them right over, or when a grain of maize maybe ten times the midget carrier's weight just won't stay put on its back.

We can hardly blame them for coveting the greens in our garden. Why lay up any old thing when there are luscious cabbage and lettuce, mango and orange leaves about? But with the garden and the work being ours, we could not just stand by and see our precious greens disappearing. The table idea was our last resort, after everything else to beat the parasols had failed. We had flushed their burrows with soapy dish water. We salted their trails with D.D.T. We lit the blow-lamp and poured fire into their dens. But if we managed to

50

flood or fumigate one store, they would work on another. They just kept to their job, laying up with all the zeal and persistence of Joseph in Egypt.

So I did what I had seen our Brazilian friends do in other parts of the River X, and made some rustic tables. The legs were forked sticks, of a kind of wood the white ants would not devour, let into the ground. The table tops were of rough wood, covered with old mats and fitted with side pieces to prevent the soil from falling off. Thanks to this device, our greens were thriving.

But a few days after our visitors left these ants discovered our secret and swarmed up these table legs in their thousands. I could not but admire their nerve and courage. Some, I noticed as I stood watching did nothing but lop leaves. Others did the carrying down the legs and along the trail to the underground store. Talk about team spirit!

What those ants had carried off in the way of lettuce leaves, they more than repaid in the lessons they had taught me. People, like ants, need to "lay up" in a storehouse open to us all through Jesus Christ— a storehouse which cannot be destroyed.

18

SALT—THE STAFF OF LIFE

Rain, rain! RAIN! How it can rain in these forests. Our Indian friends are having a hungry time, for with the rains come the mud and the mosquitoes, then the colds and the fevers. Our hunters have not been well enough to go very far in their search for fish and game. I have been very grateful for our reserve supply of canned foods.

The last fresh meat we had was a leg of armadillo and not very inviting to the appetite in its horny armour plate. When Donna Eva had done her best with it and we were ready to eat, I remembered an unopened tin of mustard in the storeroom.

"Mustard makes the meal," I quoted confidently as I opened the tin, but alas, the damp climate had turned the yellow mustard green and so mouldy that it had become useless.

"I ought to have known," I said, as we ate that uninteresting stew together. "Ground pepper goes the same way, and baking powder and even curry." Then I looked up from my plate and eyed the two big sacks of salt which lay on a shelf built high above the fire-place. "Never mind the mustard and pepper, it's the salt which matters most and we have plenty of that. Our salt will never let us down!"

Salt, like soap and paraffin, is a very big *must* in our rain-forest home, so far from shops and markets and where we have no "fridge". Were it only to make food tasty—as at home in England—very few pounds would suffice for a whole year's needs. But because we use it so much for preserving, we have to buy salt by the hundredweight.

Fish and game deteriorate very quickly in the tropics, and what is not eaten right away must be evenly sprinkled with salt and then dried in the sun if it is not to be lost. What is preserved in this way will keep indefinitely. Donna Eva knows when she goes into her larder for a piece of preserved meat or fish that she can rely on the salt to have done its work well.

I often wonder what kind of salt it was that the Lord Jesus said could lose its savour. Perhaps it was different from our sodium chloride. Maybe when exposed or left in contact with the ground it would absorb something which changed its chemical constituency and robbed it of its taste.

Whatever it was, that salt must have been in everyday use for keeping fish as well as making it tasty when put in the pot. Peter and his fishermen friends must have been expert not only in catching fish but in preserving the fish they caught. How concerned they must have been for those 153 great fishes caught by the miracle recorded for us in St. John, chapter 21, that none of them should be lost!

The "fish" that Jesus is most concerned about are people. He called those fishermen brothers to make them fishers of men, and told those same disciples to be His salt too!

Why salt as well as fishermen? Because Jesus wanted people to be kept, as well as caught, through their ministry!

There are lots of people being caught for Jesus these days. It would be wonderful if every single Christian could be a fisherman for His Lord. But however important the catching may be, we must not forget the keeping. Jesus saves and Jesus keeps, but he looks to every one of His disciples, young and old, to live and work as His "salt".

We can be the kind of Christian that attracts—bright, clean, friendly, kind and courteous, with both conversation and conduct untainted. Those who are just beginning to follow Jesus are looking to us to see if what the preachers say about a brand-new life and radiant Christianity is really true.

Our stock of sodium chloride here on the shelf will never let us down, no matter how wet or dry the weather, how dusty or smoky or damp the air, or how many months it may be lying there. But the Lord's "salt" is always a concern to Him.

It can lose its savour.

Christians can cease to be keen and out-and-out for their Lord. They can be fickle and changing in their devotion. Their testimony can lose its edge through love of self or other sin. The spirit of the world can eat its way right into their souls and take away that wholesome tang which belongs to the true salt of the earth. They lose their savour, let down the Chief Fisherman, become a hindrance and the means of good fish being lost.

19

THE TRIUMPHANT FROG

The rainy season is just ending and we are glad. The seven wet months are a dreary time for most forest dwellers, ourselves and the Indians included.

Almost alone among jungle creatures, the frog is in his element. The more it rains, the happier he seems to be and he lets everybody know how he feels. There is a swamp just outside our village and we sometimes get the impression that it is the home of a million frogs. All night long, right through the rainy season, that swamp echoes with a mighty chorus of croakers. And, strangely enough, they sound as if they are calling the Indian word for water—*n'go . . . n'go . . . n'go.*

When the rains finish, the swamp begins to dry up and, if its inhabitants are to survive, they must scatter. So away they go in search of water holes which do not dry up during the months when rain is but a dream.

Many a time, on our journeys through the forest, we have been grateful for those water-loving frogs. Travellers can get dreadfully thirsty on the trail and it often happens that it is the croaking of some lone frog which guides them to a spot where there is still water enough to dampen their parched tongues.

The frog has found water, or rain is coming, and he wants to share the good news.

Now the other day, Donna Eva called me to see a frog she had discovered trying to hide in her kitchen. It was as black as coal and as flat as a pancake. Donna Eva suggested that the poor thing had somehow been crushed. What impressed me was that crushed or no, the frog was keeping his chin up! Quite unconcerned at our presence, he hopped away into the shadows behind our five-gallon jar of drinking water, where it is not only dark but cool.

"Let him stay," pleaded Donna Eva, as I prepared to throw him out. "This is only the kitchen and, after all, even frogs need somewhere to live."

However, later in the day I was recalled by an indignant wife who had found the frog in our bedroom. From time to time the kitchen water-jar had to be taken down to the river for refilling, and this, no doubt, had disturbed him and given him undesired publicity. Hence his desire to explore the bedroom.

This seemed to be imposing on good nature, and picking up a broom, she took action and most unceremoniously brushed him out of the house altogether. As far as we were concerned, he must join the rest of his kind in their search for suitable accommodation by a water hole. Once installed, he would soon settle down and join his mates in the evening chorus of *n'go . . . n'go . . . n'go . . .* which, during the dry months must needs be on a greatly reduced scale.

However, we had not seen the last of that flat, black frog!

At supper time, I lit the pressure lamp and we sat down to a meal of boiled fish and manioc cereal, grateful for a light good enough for us to pick out the bones. Then, would you believe it, in came that frog, his chin higher than ever, as round the room he made h is way mopping up mosquitoes!

There he was, rooting them out of their hideouts in the clay walls with his long tongue. If he spotted one out of range, up he would jump and get it while still in the air!

"Good old fellow," I muttered, "There you go, crushed, sat on and kicked out, yet with no ill feeling at all, getting on with the good work while the rest of the world takes it easy!"

If a puny creature like a frog can refuse to be discouraged, if he can keep his chin up in the face of misunderstanding and opposition and not let it interfere with his programme of doing good; if he can be at his best when the weather is at its worst and never tire of sharing his good news, then surely we humans can take courage.

20

BATTLE OF THE BATS

Our house has been plagued by a whole squadron of bats. Once the light from our pressure-lamp is extinguished, there is a swishing and a swooping, a flapping and a fluttering, and the nightly invasion is on. We have been afraid lest during our sleep our fingers, elbows or toes should touch the flimsy muslin of our mosquito nets and get nipped by bat teeth! We have tried to keep them away by leaving a storm-lantern burning, but this has been ineffective.

The Indians did not seem concerned when we told them. One of them had arrowed a bat he had found sleeping in an orange tree just outside our back door.

It had a wingspread of twenty inches, and ugh, the teeth!

"But there is nothing to be afraid of," he assured us. "This kind doesn't bite. The blood-drinkers are small."

We were quite aware that most of the world's bats are harmless and live on insects and that not all our Brazilian ones are vampires. But why should those teeth have to be so big and sharp? And what attraction could the few mosquitoes in our house have for so many bats?

Then we noticed that a big bunch of bananas in our storeroom had been well nibbled overnight. Here among the Indians we get plenty of bananas. We eat them singly and we eat them by the dozen. We eat them baked and boiled. We squash them and make them into porridge, cut them in strips and fry them in oil, or dry them in the sun until they turn brown and taste like seedless figs.

"Bats like bananas too," said the Indians.

My problem was how to keep those bats away from

ours! Next day I decorated the house with tufts of sharp sword-grass, just as if it might be with holly and mistletoe at Christmas time. I thought that this might cut their wings as many a time it has cut my feet, ankles and fingers. But no. Even in the dark, the bats' built-in radar enabled them to avoid the traps hanging for them, eat their fill of ripe bananas and take off again without receiving a scratch.

Then came an Indian hunter with another suggestion. "Try prickly bobs. They get under the bats' wings and stick fast. Then they'll go away and not come back."

We tried it, but that idea did not work. The bats were there to the last, ripe banana!

I could not admit myself beaten. I would make a screened pantry, absolutely bat-proof. And meanwhile I would thank those bats for the lesson they had given me in sheer tenacity of purpose. We must take a hint from our battle with the bats and go on to beat our trials and difficulties. Whether overseas or on the home front, we Christians are called to a big task: that of making Jesus known and winning others for Him. May He keep us all from discouragement and give us something of the toughness of St. Paul.

"Knocked down but never knocked out."

"Ready for anything through the strength of the One Who lives in me."

21

TAMING WILD INDIANS

One day the Indians were looking at the pictures in some of our magazines and their eyes popped with wonder as they saw a team of elephants at work in a saw-mill, using their trunks to carry and stack huge logs.

"Why are there no elephants in our jungle to help us?" they lamented.

When I told the Indians how wild and destructive elephants can be, they wanted to know how those in the pictures are so tame and able to work so well.

I never saw an elephant tamer at work but I have read how he sends a specially trained, tame elephant to mix with those still wild and lure them into a big enclosure where they can be domesticated and their great strength and intelligence harnessed to useful ends. The Indians received my explanation with nods of approval. They have their own ways of taming things, but with Brazilian jungle creatures being so small, little skill or ingenuity is involved.

During the days when our own villagers were burning their clearings to make new forest gardens, we saw other smoke away on the horizon. When night fell, a glow in the sky told of some strange, wild group of forest nomads also preparing their forest gardens. For years such groups have terrorized the region more than elephants or lions could ever do.

How to deal with such wild Indians is a real problem. One way would be to kill them off. That is the wild-west way so frequently described in redskin and cowboy stories. But it is not the way of the Christian missionary, or yet of the present kindly and humane government of Brazil. How delighted we were when some of our own Indians volunteered to go off into the forest to try to make friends with the wild ones.

Away we saw them go with our presents of beads, fish hooks and salt. They wore clothes they had received for work done for us. They carried new bush knives with which to cut their way through the forest. But most important of all, we felt, was that they would be able to tell about the missionary white-men who have come to live in their village; how we treat the sick and teach the boys to read what the paper says. They would be able to tell of the Jesus-Way and sing our Jesus-songs.

Each day we prayed for them, for anyone going on such a venture needs to be brave as well as trustworthy. Weeks went by and we began to fear for their safety. How excited we were when they eventually returned, not only safe and sound, but bringing with them Indians we had never seen before. Our "tame" Indians were bringing in the "wild" ones!

And is that not just how God works? Chief among the tasks He has given us to do is the winning of others. Of course, we are not expected to say to them "I'm tame, you are wild. I am better than you are." We are rather to tell them what a wonderful Master we have and seek to lead them to Him. We cannot do the taming, nor does our Master expect us to try. Only His Word and His power and His love can do that. Our job is to go out and seek to bring them in for the Master's Hand to touch and to tame.

22

EAR OF THE TAPIR

On a river journey I made with four Indians, we had been living for days on snacks and were longing for a really good meal—one which would last all day and even then leave something over for supper!

As our boat rounded a bend in the river, a big animal was having a quiet bathe. "Tapir!" breathed the Indians in one breath.

The tapir is as tough-looking as his flesh makes tough eating. His head is big, hard and stream-lined, a wonderful provision for life in the jungle, for it can crash through the densest thicket.

His skin is so thick and tough that he is indifferent to thorns and stings, and even arrows and buckshot if these are shot at random. His legs are short and powerful, hoofed and very sure-footed. The cutest thing about him is a short trunk, enough to cover his mouth and leave an inch or two over. He raises it when he eats and when he whistles to his mate. When danger is in the air, sensitive as an aerial the same raised trunk sniffs around and keeps him informed.

Those Indians had not made a sound but that aerial was already alerted for danger. His big hard wedge of a head was raised, his oval ears had stiffened, while the short trunk twitched and sniffed the air. And before anyone could reach for a gun, he was away, his legs working like piston rods and his hooves making no mistake for all the slipperiness of the river bank.

"I'm going after him", whispered an Indian. "Give me the new gun and you wait here with the old one in case he takes to the water." I gave a grudging consent, because I had purchased the gun for a special friend, handed it over, and watched him scramble ashore and disappear into the jungle.

I half hoped that we had seen the last of that tapir. Once back in the river he would almost certainly escape us. He swims like an otter and the Indians tell me that he can actually walk underwater along the river bottom. However, after a few minutes, we heard a shrill tapir call, then another and another. There was a pause and then, from quite a different direction, a responding call. This was repeated, call and counter call getting nearer to each other as the minutes went by. Then suddenly, there was a bang!

When the hunter pushed his way back to the boat, it was to report a kill and to get his companions to sharpen their knives for the skinning and quartering. My own first thought, peevishly enough, was for the new gun I was wanting to return to its wrapping paper. To my dismay, I saw that the wooden ramrod was now minus its metal head! The hunter explained that he had loaded the gun in a hurry and that the ramrod head must have broken off as he had rammed the wadding on top of the charge of powder and shot. With so much meat in prospect, none of the Indians could understand why I should be so concerned about such a trifle as a broken ramrod!

When, later on, I reached the scene of the kill, I found the tapir already skinned and the tough hide serving as a mat on which the cutting up was to be done. I noticed with amazement the size of the beast, the massive head and the thickness of the skin. However could a single shot from a muzzle-loader have been so deadly?

I asked the hunter to show me the bullet hole. Glad to see me thawing out, he said with a smile, "If you want to get a tapir with a single arrow or charge of buckshot. there is only one place. You must get him in the ear. The big job is to get him turn his ear your way. That is why I gave him a call. He is a lonesome animal. He is not really wild or as tough as he looks. He took my call as being friendly. I kept calling until I got his ear. The rest was easy."

"That's true with people as well as with tapirs," I said to myself. "If I am to catch anyone for God, whether here in Brazil or at home in England, I must somehow get his ear. Behind many a tough look there can be a lonely, friendly heart, just waiting to respond to the right approach. The thing for me is to be patient, to go all out to get his ear, and then to trust God for the right word."

The hunter was poking his knife into the soft flesh just under the tapir's ear. A couple of deep probes and he felt the point touch metal. Putting in his fingers, he brought out the missing brass head of the ramrod!

"Now you can be happy again," he said with a grin. It took me only a few minutes to dig out the broken wood end and put the brass cap back where it belonged. The gun was as good as new again! And as I washed my hands after operation tapir-ear was over, I said to myself, "No wonder the tapir dropped like a stone! And if I can only remember what I have learned today about the importance of ears, I shall be more than repaid for any damage done to this muzzle-loader!"

23

JUNGLE TURNCOAT

We like our river journeys. For one thing they are restful after the pressures of life in the village. And they are interesting. Things to be seen both in the water and on the river bank enable us to forget hard seats and hot sun.

The other day we called a halt for a mid-day meal and moored our boat to a tree. One of the Indians, who was gathering a few dry sticks with which to make a camp-fire, suddenly looked up and pointed to a branch overhanging the water. At first I couldn't see anything, nor could Donna Eva, but looking very carefully at where he was pointing, we discerned a chameleon. The meaning of his name is "Lion of the Earth". To see his picture is to be reminded of a young crocodile. But the chameleon is anything but fierce, or even bold.

He was holding on to that branch as if his very life depended on it. And, as if his four legs and feet were not enough, he was making extra sure by using his long tail as a hook. How different from the playful, daring monkeys we see hanging by the tip of the tail, a hundred feet up!

We had found it hard to see him for as he lay on that branch he was as green as the leaves which almost hid him. But he is not always green. He can look anything from a dirty white to almost black, and sometimes quite brown. It is said that he is able to change colour at will, just to match his surroundings. That is because he does not like being seen. He does not want his enemies—particularly hawks—to know he is there. Another opinion is that his colour is determined, not so much as by where he happens to be, but by how he happens to feel. It depends on whether he is warm or cold, wide-awake or sleepy, scared, angry or hungry.

But in the ordinary way he looks very green and feels very cold. I once handled a live chameleon and, although the day was very warm, his body was as cold as a dog's muzzle.

64

Being a reptile, he is cold-blooded. Any warmth he wants must come from outside, which is why he spends so much time basking in the sunshine. And as he basks, he dozes. Poor fellow, should a hawk catch him unawares, or a prowling wild-cat.

It would seem that it is not the cold blood which is the cause of the chameleon's being so changeable. Warm-blooded human beings can be every bit as changeable! Wherever the chameleon is known, he has become the symbol of those who can make a quick change of opinions, attitude, political party, or even religion, just whenever it suits them.

Nobody admires a turncoat, and the kind most despised is the religious one. What a hindrance to Christianity are those who profess to be Christians but whose lives are inconsistent.

St. Peter once gave a solemn promise that he would never forsake Jesus, even though it might mean dying for Him. But that same night, Jesus was arrested and Peter, who was there, began to feel cold. There was a fire in the high priest's courtyard and he went to warm himself. But his coldness was such that no fire on earth could deal with. He was afraid. All the warmth and fervour he felt when with Jesus disappeared. His whole appearance changed with his circumstances and, when taunted, the testimony of a Christian disciple became the lying and swearing of an ungodly man.

But it only needed one look from the Lord Jesus to bring tears to Peter's eyes and a deep sense of shame and sorrow to his heart. He still believed. He still loved. But he was weak, and prone to change with changing circumstance.

Only on the Day of Pentecost did St. Peter find the fire he needed to deal with his problem. It was spiritual fire. With the other believers, he was filled with the Holy Spirit, "baptized with the Holy Ghost and fire" as Jesus had promised. Peter the fearful became a good soldier of Jesus Christ, never again to deny his Lord.

24

SNAKES ALIVE

"Snake!" is a common cry in these parts, but it never fails to alert, and a crowd soon gathers.

The other day, the shout went up from our kitchen, and I ran in to find Donna Eva pointing excitedly to a loop of snake clearly visible between two layers of the palm-leaf thatched roof. The Indian boys were quickly on the scene, some with sticks, one with a bush knife and all with plenty of noise and enthusiasm.

What shall we do? Shall it be a quick slash at the exposed coil or a well directed poke with a stick to bring it down to earth where the actual killing will be easier?

The latter is what we did, and the boy made no mistake as he brought down his stick on the scaly body. But the shouts which followed were those of disappointment. What came tumbling down to earth was not a live snake but an empty skin, light and transparent as a plastic bag.

Snakes have the habit of shedding their skins from time to time. Spiders do too. So do caterpillars when they become chrysalides, and in turn the ugly chrysalis is shed when the beautiful butterfly emerges. But when a snake sheds its skin, what emerges is just the same old enemy with a new look, a new lustre in its scales, a new gleam in its eye.

If that empty skin meant disappointment for the Indians, it meant far more for Donna Eva and me, living in that primitive house with the straw roof and clay walls which makes the best kind of hideout in the world for this enemy. When other enemies get the worst of an encounter, they will run or slink away and not return. But nobody wants a snake to get away. The only snakes you can be happy about are dead ones. The snake that gets away is soon ready to stage a come-back and with a brand new look!

So both indoors and outside, with the Indian boys to help, we cleared away everything in which the snake might be lurking. He was still alive and not too far away from the old coat he had discarded. We realized that there could be no once-for-all freedom from snakes as long as our home was in jungle-land.

It is just the same with sin and temptation. The Bible refers more than once to "that old serpent" which is Satan. We should like to think either that he does not exist or that he will never bother us, but that would be very wishful and very foolish thinking indeed.

In the story of our Lord's temptation in the wilderness Satan had in the end to retreat, a defeated foe.

But St. Luke is careful to tell us that his departure was only for a season. Time and again he returned, nothing discouraged, and always with a new look. On one occasion he used St. Peter himself as his mouthpiece, just as later on he entered into Judas Iscariot and caused him to betray Jesus to His enemies.

The only One Satan truly fears is the Lord Jesus, and safety for us lies in walking and working with Him, following closely all the time, eyes and ears alert and taking no risks.

25

CALLING THE JAGUAR

When the Indians are away fishing or hunting, the empty village at Smoking Waterfall can be a creepy place, especially at night. Above the ceaseless rumble of water tumbling over the falls comes the croaking of countless frogs, the grunts of foraging pigs, the hooting of owls and the weird cries of twittering bats.

One night, over and above the usual queer sounds, Donna Eva could make out the short, throaty grunts of a jaguar. She did not wake me, for with the stout fence around our house, and the closed bedroom door, she felt quite safe. But as she told me next morning, she was pretty confident there would be plenty of jaguar tracks to confirm her story. But for once, Donna Eva was wrong. It turned out that all the 'jaguar calls' had come from a lone hunter named Koory-ko, one of the very few men to remain behind.

In the ordinary way, the Kayapó Indians fish and hunt as a pack. Koory-ko is learning to work alone, and very successfully too. Whenever we see an Indian wanting to be different, we try to help him, for it shows that he is beginning to think, as well as act, for himself. How pleased we were the other day when we heard Koory-ko telling a visitor that he is a Jesus-hearer! That is surely a decision we can only make for ourselves.

Koory-ko is good at making things as well as decisions. At one time it was model airplanes. On one particular night he was practising on his home-made *roncadeira*, a gadget which can imitate to perfection the call of a jaguar. It is just a wooden drum, 7 inches in diameter by 15 inches long and left open at one end. Through the dried skin which closes the other end, a nail is driven into a loose wooden rod inside the drum. When this rod is coated with bees-wax and rubbed with the fingers, it causes the skin to vibrate and produce a sound so realistic that any jaguar within range takes it as coming from either a mate or a rival. It is in fact the hunter's challenge to the jaguar to come out into the open and fight!

It seemed that Koory-ko was looking for trouble as he set out in the hope of bagging a jag. While the pack was asleep by the camp fires, he paddled his canoe into the darkness to sound out his challenge. The wait was long, cold and hungry, but in the end, he heard a jaguar call back and begin to come nearer, slowly at first and then at speed. Came the moment of confrontation. Swopping his *roncadeira* for his gun, he held a flashlight against the barrel, took quick aim and pressed the trigger. The shot did not drop the jaguar right away, and he had to wait for daylight before he dare follow the blood-splashed trail to where it was lying dead.

It was a very exultant Indian who returned to the village with his trophy. As we saw the pelt and heard the story, we could see that Koory-ko's looking for trouble had been well worth while.

We saw our own need of patience and courage as we proclaim the Name of Jesus to the Indian tribe. We have been missionaries long enough to realize that, except where the Holy Spirit of God is working in the hearts of men and women, they can be satisfied with their way of life—sin, darkness and all. When pagan peoples call "Come over and help us", it is usually material benefit they have in mind and not the way of salvation from sin.

26

THE GRASS-HOPPER MIND

We were just about ready for bed one night when Donna Eva pointed to a big green insect perched on the mosquito netting. The mosquitoes were buzzing around and we were wanting to get that net between us and their stabbing probosces. And now there was this suspicious-looking creature, seated on the net and looking as if he were all set for eating a hole in the net so that the hungry mosquitoes could get in and at us.

Flashing the light, I could see that it was only a Brazilian grass-hopper. Insects in Brazil are quite in keeping with the size of the country and grass-hoppers are no exception. He was much bigger than the kind we have at home, but a grass-hopper for all that.

"Nothing to be afraid of," I called out. "Only rats, beetles and white-ants will damage our net. The grass-hopper only eats green leaves." Donna Eva was not to be easily convinced. "That may be true," she said, "but do put him out of our bedroom. There is no grass in here."

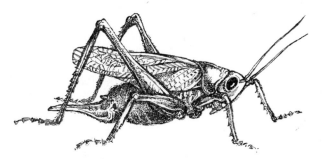

So I gave the net a shake as I do when I want to clean the bits of straw the wind blows down from our thatched roof. The grass-hopper was quite unmoved by my shaking. I then gave him a flick, as if he were a wasp, fly or beetle. He did not budge. Finding an old magazine, I made it into a roll and gave him a swipe. But never an inch did he retreat. Finally, I seized him between my thumb and forefinger and pulled. Even then, the grass-hopper was most reluctant to let go.

Then I noticed that his legs were fitted with grips like the teeth of a saw—not for cutting, but for holding on.

Seeing himself overpowered, the grass-hopper hopped, and a real good hop it was. I went after him to see that he hopped again until he was right out of the house. Imagine my surprise to find him waiting for me, with his head turned my way. Far from waiting to be poked in the back, he was already turned right round and facing whatever might be coming, like a boxer coming in for another round. I poked him again, and again he hopped but made another complete turn in mid-air, so that when he landed, he was already facing his foe!

"You're game and no mistake," I muttered. "Your motto seems to be 'Only give way when you have to, and even then, keep facing the enemy'."

Did you ever come across the word "back-slide"?

A back-slider is a professing Christian who doesn't stand firm when tempted and tested, but gives up and goes back. Now whatever unkind things may be said of the grass-hopper, he cannot back-slide. His legs were built for standing, not sliding. His direction is forward, not backward. If we see him hopping around, he is looking for something. He will hop around until he finds it. Then he stays put. He plants his feet and those non-skid legs of his, and there is no moving him until he is through. Hit him, beat him, knock him down or chase him out, he is tough. When he moves, it is forward. He is game. When he comes up again, he is facing the enemy. That is what I have seen in these Brazilian grass-hoppers.

There was a time when great multitudes followed the Lord Jesus because He had fed them with loaves and fishes. When later He applied the lesson and spoke to them of the Living Bread and of Eternal Life, the crowds disappeared. We read that many went back

and walked no more with Him. (St. John 6:66–69).
Turning to His disciples, Jesus asked them point-blank
whether they would go too.

Peter replied for them all: "Lord, to whom shall we
go? Thou hast the words of eternal life. And we believe
that Thou are that Christ, the Son of the Living God."

They were not casual Christians.

They were not Christians for the sake of loaves and
fishes.

They wanted Eternal Life, and, having found that in
the Lord Jesus, they were His for ever.

27

NEW NAME FOR FROG EYES

Bree-Not is the name of an Indian girl-mother at
Smoking Waterfall. She doesn't know how old she is.
She cannot count because there are no numbers in the
tribal language. She is about fifteen years old and often
comes to see us, with Black Water, her baby boy,
perched in a strip of tree bark knotted to make a sling
and hung over her shoulder. Both mother and baby
have lovely dark eyes, brown skin and jet black hair.
Baby has wooden plugs like fat cigars pushed through
the lobes of his ears, and in a wee hole bored through
his lower lip is an inch of cotton thread with a button
tied to one end and couple of white beads to the other.

One day Bree-Not came along with a small bunch of
bananas to exchange for a razor blade.

"I want to shave Black Water's eyebrows," she
explained.

There were hardly any brows to shave and I noticed
that every single eyelash had been removed. I was not

surprised at this, since it is an Indian custom. From the tiniest baby to the oldest warrior or squaw, all lashes are plucked out. Little eyes squirm in their sockets during the process, but they soon get used to it and quite small boys and girls are able to do it for themselves.

"Black Water's eyes are so nice," I said. "Why don't you leave them alone?"

"Eye hairs are ugly," she answered. "You shave your chin, we shave our eyebrows. We want our babies to see properly as we do."

There is no answering that kind of argument. At least, as regards the shaved brows. The plucked lashes are a different matter. Donna Eva is often called to treat eyes where the plucking has caused inflammation.

"You don't have to go into the forest like we do," she went on. "We walk through the forest every day and our eyes need to be wide awake all the time."

I had heard it all before. The Indians say that lashes would prevent them from seeing upwards and down-wards, forwards and sideways all at the same time!

"Tell you what," I suggested. "If Black Water only had 'bree not' he would really be able to look in all directions without turning his head!" At this there was a roar of laughter from the other Indians present. Bree-Not just bowed her pretty head and giggled for she knew I was teasing her about her name.

When she was born, there was no careful name-choosing as when our children are born. There was nothing glamorous like some of the names we associate with Indian girls—Laughing Water, Minne-haha, Pocahontas. Tradition demanded that she be named after her grandma—Bree-Not. And in the language of the Kayapó tribe, Bree-Not means Frog Eyes!

Now frog eyes have neither lashes to pluck nor brows to shave. And they are set in what look like cone-shaped turrets in which the eye itself is just visible at the top. No need for a frog to peep through the corner of an eye when it wants to look sideways. It has a marvellous range of vision.

Indians can do wonders with the eyes they have and that without spectacles, even in old age. They can look down to avoid treading on thorns or snakes and at the same time be looking up for birds and honey bees. They can be looking ahead so as not to miss the trail, and sideways to make sure there is no jaguar waiting to jump on them from behind a tree. They also have a way of having one eye on the missionary nurse, with her medicines, and the other on the witch-doctor and his charms. They can have one eye on the Jesus Way and the other on the old ways of superstition and sin. Bree-Not became a 'Jesus-hearer', as the Indians call Christians. When she was baptized, she was given a new name more in keeping with the new way of life she now follows. The name chosen is Amanda, meaning 'Worthy of love'. Amanda's dark eyes shine all the brighter for the new light, life and love that Jesus gives.

28

GUIDANCE FROM THE GECKO

On a Saturday morning, Donna Eva and Jess were washing up the breakfast things. Jim and his friend Simon were stacking firewood. I was out in the village.

Our kitchen is ten paces from the dining room where the china is kept in a home-made cupboard. Jess brought in a trayful of washed cups, saucers and plates, and was arranging them on the shelves when she spotted what she took to be chewing gum—it was white, rounded and apparently sugar-coated as she had so often seen—and tested—before.

She popped it into her mouth and promptly gave a squeal that brought Donna Eva dashing along the corridor from the kitchen and Jim and Simon from the wood-pile. They found Jess quite speechless and pointing to a creature like a baby crocodile which lay quivering on the floor. Hard by it lay the broken shell of the "chewing gum"!

"It looked for all the world like a sweet," breathed Jess, "but when I put my teeth into it, out came that animal!"

It was an egg, of course. Jim had found it in a wall which was being repaired and had taken it into the house to ask me whether it belonged to bird or snake. The "animal" which had popped out was a baby gecko, a member of the lizard family.

When night fell, there was more than the usual interest in the geckos which, as we lit the pressure lamp, came creeping down the walls from their hiding places in the roof. Only three or four inches long, they are miracles for speed, agility and holding on. Their feet are like hands, complete with five fingers, all of which are needed for the very tricky business of running up and down sheer wall at high speed without falling. Whenever a fly, moth or mosquito touched down for a few moments within range of the pressure-lamp's bright light, two or three geckos would creep in from different directions, advancing so slowly and silently that the victims never suspected their presence. The first gecko to get within range would make a lightning pounce and with a quick snap of its tiny jaws, the catch would be complete.

The strange thing about geckos is that you rarely see them at work away from a good light and a smooth wall. We have lots of insects in this home of ours, but very few in comparison with what the Indians have to contend with in their lodges and primitive houses with straw roofs, rough, clay walls and only say a smoky paraffin lamp at night. Where walls are smoothed off and given a coat of whitewash like ours, there are few places where insects can hide away and go to sleep in the daytime, so out they must go. But in the nooks and crannies of those hovels, the walls are simply alive with insects of all kinds, by day as well as by night. Yet in such houses, from my own observation, geckos seem few and far between. What hunting is done at all, is done by the spiders, and the driver ants.

No doubt geckos existed long before men learned to smooth their walls with plaster and illuminate their houses with pressure-lamps and electric light. The gecko pioneers may have been tough but it seems to me that with the progress in the way of civilized homes, they lost the spirit of adventure and began to look round for an easier time. Why work in rough, hard places when one can live quite usefully in some well-lit, comfortable spot where the going is easier on hands and feet?

The gecko is small and exceeding wise, but it seems to me a pretty worldly kind of wisdom, the kind which is only thinking about self. He is willing to work—and work hard—but with a preference for the easy, straight-forward task, and right in the limelight. That is all very well for a mere insect (or is it a reptile?) which cannot be expected to do other than follow its own instincts, but it is surely not good enough for Christians wanting to serve their Saviour and Lord to the utmost. There is plenty to do in Church and Sunday School, but how much more outside?

At family prayers that night, still thinking about Jess's gecko, we read together our Lord's testimony concerning John the Baptist. "What went ye out into the wilderness for to see? A reed shaken in the wind? A man clothed in soft raiment? Behold, they that wear soft clothing are in kings' houses."

What a tough pioneer was John the Baptist! He preferred the wilderness to the king's court, and yet, when the need arose, he was quite ready to face Herod and reprove his sinful ways. For John, it was the life of discipline, hardship and sacrifice. He did not hold back from burning himself right out for God.

29

TIP FROM THE TERMITES

Returning to the village after weeks of river travel, we had a surprise when we opened our front door and the shuttered windows. Perched on top of the low wall which separates living room and bedroom, was an unsightly growth as big as a football. Exclaimed Donna Eva, who was the first to see it, "Isn't that a nest of those white ants you write your stories about? Root them out before they bring the house down!"

There was no danger, I assured her. The walls are of puddled clay and the only thing that white ants destroy is the wooden reinforcing which had really served its purpose once the clay had hardened. Seeing that to demolish the ant-hill would make a mess in both rooms, we decided to let it stay until a more convenient time.

Weeks passed and then, one very wet evening, we saw a multitude of strange insects flying around. Thinking they were coming in from outside, we hurriedly closed doors and windows, but it made no difference. They were parachuting down from that nest on top of the wall! The whole house was at their mercy, for with there being no ceilings, they could fly over the walls from one room to another. They were swarming everywhere.

I had that nest down in a hurry, regardless of the mess it made, and found it alive with white ants all sprouting wings in readiness for their mass descent to earth. It did not take long to destroy them and clean up the mess, after which doors and windows were opened again. But now the things began to come in from outside. At that very same hour, every ant-hill in the neighbourhood was unloading its winged commandos! One would have thought those termites were in league with each other and following the carefully made plans of a supreme command. Down they swarmed from nests in the forks of trees. Up they came from ant-hills on the ground.

From a window we watched the swallows and night-jars mopping them up in mid air. Our neighbours' chickens were eating their fill. Mud and puddles destroyed untold thousands. But still they came. At lighting-up time they were everywhere. They fluttered round our pressure lamps. They fell in the soup and spoiled our evening meal. They got in Donna Eva's hair and crawled down the open neck of my shirt. We swatted them with rolled newspapers and bombarded them with Flit. And still they came!

It was the termites' mammoth reproduction act, their annual drive to found new colonies. How any of them survive is a miracle, but survive they do. As they contact Mother Earth, they shed their flimsy wings and the parachutists become infantrymen. They dig in, get under cover, link up, advance in single file and, in next to no time, new colonies of white ants are formed all over the place.

Wrapping my head in a towel and sipping my tea with the saucer covering the cup, I surprised Donna Eva by telling her that I had often had the same kind of feeling when at home in England!

"These termites," I explained, "are a kind of parable. I often found my eyes, ears, and mind and even home invaded by hosts of silly little things which used to come parachuting down on me from the hoardings, or bouncing up at me from newspapers and magazines or being shot at me from T.V. screens. At times the very air seemed alive with them—advertisements for this, that and the other and all making the most fantastic claims."

I must have sounded very enthusiastic.

"Commerce knows all about this termite technique," I went on. "Why cannot we Christians challenge the world in the same way? The apostles not only filled Jerusalem with their doctrine but turned the world upside down! God bless the people who today are attempting really big things for God!"

"Yes, God bless them indeed," said Donna Eva. And then, after a little pause, "But we cannot all do things in a big way, can we?"

I have to admit that she is right. So out here we keep on with our God-given task of making Jesus known to Indians who never saw a poster, could not read a tract, have no radio, and would never have had a Christian hymn or verse of Scripture had we not come.

30

WHAT TOUCAN DO!

Saying goodbye to Brazil has not been easy. We have many friends here and there has been much to see to before we can get away on our furlough. We were glad to be able to arrange a final outing to the Para Zoo to see once again all the queer animals there: tapirs and turtles, anteaters and armadillos, sloths and jaguars, and lots more besides.

Everything but the jaguars and birds of prey seem to be quite happy, with regular meals, good shelter, freedom from fear, and the sheer fun of seeing so many human beings. Surely far better than life in the jungle.

Perhaps most at home are the toucans, those marvellously coloured birds with the outsize bills. Most of them have bright blue feet with rings exactly the same hue around their eyes. Some have white bibs, some gaudy yellow, with here and there a red splash. Their black and white fan tails are long, their wings short. But it's always the curved beak you notice most, red or yellow—or both—and huge out of all proportion to the rest of its cute little body.

The toucan has always appeared to me as being severely handicapped for life in the wilds. However he manages to survive in those jungle tree tops is a miracle.

Hawks are so many, so fast and always so hungry and relentless. For the toucan, with his beak so big and his coat so gay, there can never be any hiding, no pretending to be foliage or a knot of wood. His beak is merely for swallowing palm berries as big and as hard as marbles and is too unwieldy to be much use as a weapon, although he certainly can nip unwary fingers when he wants to. As for outflying an enemy, that is out of the question for the toucan is not in the fighter class either for speed or acrobatics. For him no lovely poise in the air, no imposing wingspread. His design seems to contradict all the laws of aerodynamics.

Yet fly he does, just as he manages to keep so fit and look so smart always. Of course, he cannot soar to great heights like the eagle and vulture. He could never tackle an ocean flight like the swallow, nor could he even attempt the shooting-star tactics of a hawk. No, he has to go slow, to look well ahead, to think things out before he takes off, and to plan all his flights in easy stages.

And, believe me, he always makes it. Away he goes, alternately flapping his wings and gliding towards the next cluster of palm trees. calling the while, "Tou-can, tou-can, tou-can". That's how he gets his name.

Now, *tou* not only rhymes with *you*, it actually means *you* in the Brazilian language, although we write it *tu*. So if only you have ears to hear, you can hear the toucan calling "You-can, you-can, yes, you-can".

There he goes, overcoming his handicaps and limitations, making the most of what God has given him, going ahead cheerfully and confidently, getting there himself and calling down, "You-can, you-can, yes, you-can too!"

Many a time, during our years in the Amazon rain forests, Donna Eva and I have felt handicapped and quite unequal to the task before us. To face the constant journeys, sometimes by plane, yes, but more often than not by river and forest trail; to endure the climate with its heat, damp, mosquitoes and malaria; to maintain a many-sided missionary witness— preaching and teaching, healing the sick and feeding the hungry; building and repairing, translating, composing and recording; working in three languages all the time.

Sometimes we have thought how much easier it was for St. Paul to be a pioneer, with no language study necessary, no family to plan for on his missionary journeys, no children to educate. But if the great apostle was able to do so much for God, it was not just because he was single and a lone pioneer by nature— not because of his natural gifts and qualifications. Here in his own words is the great secret of his success. "I can do all things THROUGH CHRIST which strengtheneth me." And isn't that as good as saying

"And if I can, then you can too"?

So we look back and see how the Lord has been with us. His goodness and mercy have followed us all the way, giving us victory over all kinds of circumstances, in spite of our weakness and the odds against us.

The God who calls you and me is the God who enables. Jesus said, "Follow Me and I will MAKE YOU. . . . !" And with Him to help you, you-can . . . . you-can . . . . yes, you-can!

There's no ceiling to what toucan do!